W

OF THEM

BERRI

The "Fishermen's Pier Team"

Chris Suhr, Sue Minchinton, Demetris Avraam, Katrina Hunt, Graeme Goldsworthy

Mocktail Magic

R&R PUBLISHING

Graeme Goldsworthy's

101 MOCKTAILS

TECHNIQUES, RECIPES AND VARIATIONS

Cheers Without Fears

Drinking That Won't Cloud Your Thinking

R&R PUBLISHING

R & R Publishing
First published in 1992 by
R & R Publishing
12 Treeview Place, Epping, NSW 2121

Publisher: Richard Carroll
Cover Design: Jon Terpstra
Data Entry: Lynette Carroll
Photography: John Bolton
Stylist: Carol Reilly
Mocktail Development: Chris Suhr
Mocktail Presentation: Demetris Avraam
Photographic Assistants: Katrina Hunt
: Sue Minchinton

National Library of Australia cataloguing in publication data

Goldsworthy, Graeme, 1937 -
Graeme Goldsworthy's 101 Mocktails

Includes index.
ISBN: 1 875655 01 8

1. Beverages 2 Entertaining. I Title. II. Title: 101 mocktails.
III. Title: One hundred and one mocktails.

641.26

First Edition June 1992

Computer Typeset in Times Roman by
R & R Publishing
Printed by: Canberra Press

Table of Contents

Forward by
The Victorian Minister for Transport,
The Hon. Peter Spyker.

It is no secret that "If you drink, then drive, you're a bloody idiot", but if you drink Mocktails, then drive, you're being responsible.

101 Mocktails, is an innovative and interesting collection of delicious non-alcoholic cocktails. They are terrific drinks that everyone can enjoy, putting anyone in a party mood without challenging the random breath tester.

The Victorian Government's hard hitting advertising campaigns against drink driving and increased random breath testing program, have made drink driving unacceptable in the community. These initiatives have assisted in reducing the road toll to the lowest figure on record.

Any measure that assist in reducing the road toll and road trauma even further is a positive measure; *101 Mocktails* is another positive and delicious step.

Increasingly, people are becoming more responsible about drink-driving. People are leaving their cars at home, taking taxis or organising non-drinking friends to drive.

Low-alcohol beers have become very popular and now Mocktails are another safe alternative at the bar.

Mocktails are a terrific alternative to cocktails which prove you do not need to consume alcohol in order to have a great time.

So if you intend drinking cocktails, think about making it a Mocktail.

Peter Spyker
VICTORIAN MINISTER FOR TRANSPORT

Introduction

Welcome to the exciting drink sensation of "Mocktails".

With the great, fresh taste of Berri juices and nectars as a base, these recipes have been gleaned from around Australia.

Capturing the very character and colour of this great land of ours, "Mocktails" reflect the growing trend away from alcohol based drinks.

Summer or Winter, Barbeque or Party, whatever the occasion, any time is the right time for a "Mocktail".

Not only are "Mocktails" fun, they are packed with the natural goodness of real Australian fruit, processed by Berrivale, the country's largest and most respected producer.

Try the various recipes with your friends. Invent your own "Mocktails", the possibilities are endless, but the most important thing is to have fun.

Happy "Mocktailing".

Peter Wood
Managing Director
Berrivale Orchards

Introduction To Mocktail Magic

Welcome to this first edition of "101 Mocktails", where the pleasurable pastime of mixing and drinking delicious non-alcoholic Mocktails is presented for your enjoyment.

If drinking Mocktails in a bar or cocktail lounge, it is always good advice to ask your bar attendant what ingredients he has available and his knowledge of mixing Mocktails. You may feel like a sweet, dry or creamy Mocktail, of which there are a number of suggestions in this book.

It is always delightful to experiment with the mixing and drinking of Mocktails at home. There are myriads of mixing ideas you may try. This book has been designed to get the juices running and provide the nucleus of a much greater range of non-alcoholic drinks.

You may ask, "What are Mocktails"? It means, quite simply, a "mock cocktail", a non-alcoholic beverage which replaces a traditional mixed drink. Mocktails have been around for years. They were once considered drinks only for " kids", real men were supposed to drink the "real stuff". For those of us who grew up from the 40s through early 80s, you will know what I mean. Remember how people thought you were "different" because you didn't drink, or only drank alcohol based drinks occasionally? Well, some amazing changes have taken place over the past few years. You are no longer a social outcaste if you prefer alternatives to alcohol, or if you only drink light beer.

Possibly, since the arrival of random breath testing, social drinking has been revolutionised. No longer is it mandatory to have that "one for the road". It is obvious to all of us that alcohol and driving do not mix. This is a prime example of when a Mocktail is both desirable and an obvious alternative. I know that when I am dining out and have to drive home, I am very conscious of my alcohol consumption, and yet find that straight fruit juice or carbonated soft drinks are boring. Mocktails provide the sensory stimulus when dining out, without the inherent danger of alcohol in a drink driving situation.

From a simple fruit juice, make a wonderful, fruity, mixture of delicious tastes, just by adding a little of another variety, or a little milk or cream, even ice cream. Blend in solid fruit with the juice or milk mixture. The ideas are endless.

I would particularly like to thank several people for their hard work and dedication in helping me compile this book, "101 Mocktails".

Firstly, to Chris Suhr at the Gordon Technical College, Geelong, for his enthusiasm and hard work. To Demitris Avraam, head waiter at Fishermen's Pier for some 15 years, well known to thousands of patrons for his fine Mocktail making and his willingness to make this book so successful. Rowan Sapwell, Manager, Fishermen's Pier, who assisted in the origination of many of the Mocktail recipes; Sue Minchinton and Katrina Hunt, hostesses at Fishermen's Pier, for their help in the preparation of the Mocktail photography. A special thank-you to the many thousands of customers at Fishermen's Pier who have enjoyed and tasted so many of our Mocktails over the last 10 years.

Graeme Goldsworthy, June 1992

General Hints on Mocktails:

A Mocktail is a non-alcoholic drink prepared from a variety of ingredients. The possible combinations are endless and only limited by your imagination and the range of available ingredients.

* Naturally fresh fruit juices are preferable to canned, bottled or concentrated forms but this is not always possible nor perhaps desirable in the commercial situation where consistency of the finished product and accurate costing are essential.

* Sugar syrup (Gomme Syrup) is called for in many drink recipes but unfortunately this is not readily available in Australia. It is quite easy to make your own by covering two cups of sugar with boiling water in a small saucepan and stirring gently until all the sugar is dissolved. Refrigerate in a glass jar or bottle. You can even make your own sweet and sour mix by combining the sugar syrup with fresh lemon juice.

  Putting a teaspoon of sugar into a Mocktail is just plain lazy, it does not do the job properly, as the sugar does not dissolve.

* Cans of fruit juice, and other ingredients, once opened must be emptied and stored into glass or plastic containers for longer storage life. Always use good quality products, not cheap ones. You always get what you pay for and cheap drinks always taste cheap. Juices must never be used if under 50% natural, as they water the Mocktail down.

* Egg white powder (Albumen) can be substituted for fresh egg white. It is available from most major supermarkets. Half a teaspoon is approximately equivalent to half an egg white.

* Small cans or bottles of juices and carbonated beverages are preferable to 750 mls sizes or larger because they maintain the freshness and effervescence and are less wasteful.

* Crushed ice can be made by wrapping cubed ice in a heavy plastic bag then hitting it with a rolling pin on a solid surface. I prefer to crush the ice by putting the cubes into a blender with sufficient water to just cover the cubes and blend for a short time at high speed, then just drain the water off.

* Cleanliness is always an important factor when mixing drinks, be it in the home or a restaurant bar. It is essential to clean the equipment you are using as well as the bar area as you mix drinks or you will soon find yourself surrounded by mess or lacking any clean utensils to prepare the next drink.

* One golden rule with cocktails or mocktails is that any carbonated soft drinks must be poured in last, never shaken or blended. Don't be frightened to experiment, that's how all mixed drinks are created.

Methods of Mixing Mocktails

Nearly all Mocktails are mixed using one of the four methods below:-

1. Shake **2.** Stir
3. Build **4.** Blend

1. Shake:

To shake is to mix a Mocktail by shaking it in a cocktail shaker by hand. Mocktails using ingredients that do not mix easily with each other should be shaken, such things as juices, egg whites, cream, sugar syrups etc. American shakers are best.

First, fill the glass part of the shaker three quarters full with ice, then pour the ingredients on top of the ice. Pour the contents of the glass into the metal part of the shaker and shake vigorously for about ten seconds. Take the glass section out and, using a Hawthorn strainer, strain into the Mocktail glass.

2. Stir:

To stir a Mocktail is to mix the ingredients by stirring them with ice in a mixing glass and then straining them into a chilled Mocktail glass. (NB. The glass part of the American shaker will do well for this.)

3. Build:

To build a Mocktail is to mix the ingredients in the glass that the Mocktail is to be served in, floating one on top of the other. Typical built Mocktails are the long fruit juice or carbonated water types. In some cases a swizzle stick is put into the drink to mix the ingredients after it has been presented.

4. Blend:

To blend a Mocktail is to mix the ingredients using an electric blender. It is used to blend fresh or canned fruit together with fruit juices. Ice should always be added last and fruit should be cut into small pieces instead of dropping it in whole. Ideally, the blender should be on for at least 20 seconds. Too many people do not blend long enough and consequential ice and fruit lumps are left with the Mocktail then needing to be strained.

Techniques in Making Mocktails

1. Shake and pour:

When you have finished shaking the Mocktail, it can be poured straight into the glass, ice cubes as well. This eliminates straining and is usually done when pouring into long glasses and sometimes old fashioned type glasses.

2. Shake and strain:

When you have finished shaking, you may use a Hawthorn strainer (available from all major department stores), to stop the ice going into the glass, usually because the glass is too small.

3. Float ingredients:

This is usually done after the Mocktail has been made; always pour, *not* over the back of a spoon as everybody suggests, but into the dish of the spoon while resting it on top of the Mocktail; that way the ingredients do not slide down the spoon and into the drink, but when the spoon fills they gently flow out of the spoon and onto the Mocktail.

Techniques in Making Mocktails (Cont)

4. Muddling:
This is when sugar cubes or mint leaves are crushed to extract the flavour or dissolve the sugar more easily. The muddler is the flat knob at the top of the spoon handle. The spoon is reversed and the flat end is used to crush the cubes or leaves. Very rarely used these days as most bar attendants cheat and use sugar syrup instead.

5. Frosting (sugar and salt rims):
This technique is used to coat the rim of the glass with either salt or sugar. A lemon slice is used for salt and an orange slice is used for sugar.

The glass is held by the stem and upturned, a lemon slice is then rubbed around *only* the rim of the glass. When the rim has been coated with juice it is rested on a plate containing salt or sugar and the glass slightly turned so that it sticks to the glass.

Do not push the glass too deeply into the salt or sugar otherwise too much adheres to the glass.

Desiccated coconut is also a delight when frosted, try it I am sure you will like it.

To achieve colour affects , put a small amount of grenadine or vegetable colouring in a plate and coat the rim of the glass then gently place in the sugar. The grenadine absorbs the sugar and turns it pink. This is much easier than mixing grenadine with sugar and then trying to get it to stick to the glass.

Ice:

Ice is probably the most important part of Mocktails. It is used in *nearly* all Mocktails. Consequently ice must be good, clean and fresh at all times.

The small squared cubes of ice are by far the best for chilling and mixing in your Mocktails. Never recycle ice for more than one Mocktail. If crushed ice is called for then just fold some into a clean linen cloth and either smash it against a concrete wall or floor or hit it with a bottle. Very primitive, but it works well and is fast.

A blender can also make crushed ice but the secret is to half fill the blender with ice and then pour water into the blender till it reaches the level of the ice. Blend for about 30 seconds, strain out the water and you have perfectly crushed ice.

Never use ice from last night that has been left, as it absorbs smoke and other odours from the room that will taint drinks and spoil them, so remember, fresh is best.

Glassware:

A brief description of common commercial glassware follows which will form the basis for the recipes in this book.

Old fashioned	=	200ml, 210ml, 290ml
Hi-Ball Glass	=	270ml, 330ml
Fancy Hi-Ball Glass	=	220ml, 350ml, 470ml
Footed Hi-Ball Glass	=	270ml, 300ml
Martini Glass	=	90 ml
Champagne Flute	=	170ml
Tulip Champagne Flute	=	260ml, 170ml
Baccus Wine Glass	=	200ml
Salud Grande Glass	=	290ml
Poco Grande Glass	=	290ml, 390ml
Viva Grande Glass	=	380ml
Fiesta Grande Glass	=	350ml, 490ml
Hurricane Glass	=	230ml, 440ml, 650ml
Margarita Glass	=	260ml

The range of glasses supplied and used in this book were provided by, Phillip Lazarus Pty. Ltd.-Australian agents for Libbey Glass of America and Crown Glassware-Hospitality Glassware Collection.

Mocktails can be poured into glass but the size of the glass is matched to the type of drink and of course to enhance the appearance of the drink.

1. Large hi-ball or hurricane glasses for long cool refreshing drinks particularly in hot climates.
2. Cocktail or old fashioned glasses for short, sharp drinks.
3. Martini, champagne saucers or flutes, for creamy after dinner type drinks.

One basic rule should apply and that is, use *no* coloured glasses as they spoil the appearance of Mocktails.

The stem of the glass has been designed to be held, leaving the bowl free of marks and germs, so that you may enjoy your drink.

All Mocktail glasses should be kept in a refrigerator or filled with ice while you are preparing the Mocktails in order to chill the glass.

An appealing affect on a 90ml glass can be achieved by running the glass under cold water and then placing it in the freezer. Mind you, if you are one of the lucky ones with plenty of refrigeration space, keep all cocktail glasses refrigerated, it really makes a difference.

Drink Categories:

Aperitif or Dry: As the name suggests, these Mocktails are not sweet but more of a piquant or sharp flavour. These are ideal for pre-dinner or to drink in hot weather as they quench the thirst far better than sweet drinks.

Sweet: These Mocktails are generally sweetened to some degree with sugar or sugar products or have a large sweet fruit juice component. These drinks are perhaps best suited for consumption towards the end of a meal or maybe for those people with a sweet tooth.

Creamy: The use of cream, milk, egg white, ice cream, coconut milk and coconut cream, give a creamy texture and full flavour to these drinks.

Garnishes and Juices

Banana
Celery
Cucumber
Lemons
Limes
Mint leaves
Olives
Celery salt
Chocolate flake
Cinnamon
Fresh eggs
Fresh single cream
Fresh milk
Apple
Carbonated waters
Coconut Cream
Lemon - pure
Orange
Tomato
Onions
Oranges
Pineapple
Red Maraschino cherries
Rockmelon
Strawberries
Canned fruit
Nutmeg
Pepper
Salt
Sugar and sugar cubes
Tabasco sauce
Worcestershire sauce
Orange and Mango
Pineapple
Sugar syrup
Canned nectars
Canned pulps
Crushed pineapple

Claytons Tonic:

A distinctive Australian product, it is a non-alcoholic drink, made from African cola nuts, citrus essences and hop bitters.

Garnishes & Novelties:

Simplicity is the most important fact to keep in mind when garnishing Mocktails. Do not overdo the garnish; make it striking, but if you can't get near the Mocktail to drink it then you have failed. Tall refreshing drinks tend to have more garnish as the glass is larger. A swizzle stick should be served nearly always in long Mocktails. Straws are always served for a lady, but optional for a man.

Plastic animals, umbrellas, fans and a whole variety of goods are now available to garnish with, which are designed to make the finished drink very attractive and exciting.

Essential Equipment for a Mocktail Bar

Cocktail shaker
Hawthorn strainer
Mixing glass
Spoon with muddler
Electric blender
Knife
Cutting board
Measures (jiggers)
Can opener
Novelties
Waiter's friend corkscrew
Bottle openers
Ice scoop
Ice bucket
Free pourers
Swizzle sticks
Straws
Coasters and napkins
Hand cloths for cleaning glasses

Equipment:

* ***Blender:*** There is a large range of both domestic and commercial blenders and food processors that are suitable for the blending of drinks. Do not over fill them nor use a large food processor to try and mix one drink. (The blades may not come into contact with the liquid sufficiently.)

* ***Cocktail Shaker:*** There are basically two styles. The first is called a Standard Shaker and is composed of three parts; the bowl, the top with an inbuilt strainer and a lid. The second is called the Boston Shaker and is of two parts. They are two similar sized bowls, one of stainless steel, the other of thick glass. The glass portion also doubles a s mixing glass.

* ***Measure:*** A simple device, sometimes called an eggcup measure. Generally made of stainless steel and with both half measure (15 mls) and full measure (30 mls) sections. It is important to use a measure to a consistent product unless of course you are a very experienced bar attendant capable of extremely accurate free pouring.

* ***Mixing Spoon:*** A long handled stainless steel spoon with a bowl size similar to a teaspoon but having a handle approximately 20 cm

* ***Ice Scoop or Ice Spoon:*** Either work well but I prefer the perforated ice spoon which prevents any water being accidently added to the Mocktail.

* ***Strainer:*** Used with both the Boston shaker and blender. It is called a "Hawthorn Strainer" (no! I do not know why it is not called a "Cats" strainer) and is available at all large department stores. It quickly strains the ice from your Mocktail and can be used with one hand holding both shaker and strainer.

Equipment (Continued):

* *Cocktail Sticks:* Similar to toothpicks and are available in plastic and wood
* *Straws*: A variety of styles are available; long, short (cocktail straws), with or without bends and in a multitude of colours.

* *Novelties:* Various fun products to attach to the glass or garnish to enhance the appearance of the drink. For example: small paper unbrellas, plastic animal and human shapes, swizzle sticks to stir the drink with, etc. Many of these have the restaurant or hotel logo imprinted on them for marketing and souvenir purposes. Beware the glass swizzle stocks that are available in stores. They may be suitable in a domestic situation but in a busy commercial scene they are liable to break, leaving splinters of glass in the drink.
* *Juicer:* There are many styles in a range of prices, all of which perform the job required.

* *Chopping Board:* Any style of chopping board is suitable but in the commercial situation, the plastic ones are less liable to absorb odours.

* *Bar Knives:* Two would be required. A large 20 cm knife for cutting pineapples and other large fruits, a small knife of approximately 10 cm for cutting standard garnishes.

* *Grater:* A small plastic or steel grater to be used for grating chocolate.

* *Zester:* A chefs speciality knife to obtain strips of citrus fruit zest without the bitter pith underneath the peel.

NB: The extent to which one stocks a bar with the above equipment depends on the amount of cocktails or Mocktails one has to prepare at a given time. For home use, not all of the equipment listed above would be required and a certain amount of improvisation would be used. Commercially, all of the above and, in fact, multiple numbers of some items would needed.

Ingredients:

Fruit and Fruit Juices:

Lemons, oranges, limes, strawberries, raspberries, blueberries, kiwi fruit, watermelons, canteloupe, rockmelons, pineapples, mangoes, peaches, apples, plums, grapes, apricots, bananas, tomatoes and various nectars and fruit pulps.

Dairy Products:

Milk, cream, ice cream (chocolate, strawberry, vanilla), yoghurt

Fruit Cordials:

Lemon, lime, raspberry and grenadine (from pomegranetes)

Carbonated Drinks:

Lemonade, dry ginger ale, tonic water, bitter lemon, soda water, cola, ginger beer.

Miscellaneous Ingredients:

Chocolate, eggs, honey, Claytons tonic, coconut cream, sugar, sugar cubes, sugar syrup, celery, carrots.

Garnishes:

These are added to enhance the appearance of the Mocktail but do not go overboard. A striking appearance would be achieved with simplicity rather than a fruit salad effect. I have seen some drinks that you cannot even get your mouth near because of all the bits and pieces attached to the glass.

Cocktail cherries (with or without stem)
Stuffed Olives
Green Olives
Black Olives
Celery Stick (with the top leaf section attached)
Mint Leaves
Carrots (with tops on)
Spices (salt, pepper, celery salt, nutmeg, cinnamon stick)
Sauces (Tabasco sauce, Worcestershire sauce)
Fruit (slices and peel of various fruits)
Desiccated coconut

Chapter 1

APERITIF or DRY

Ideal for pre-dinner
or to drink in hot weather
as they quench
the thirst far better
than the sweeter variety.

ANDY WILLIAMS

METHOD:	Shake with Ice and Pour
GLASS:	290ml Old Fashioned Glass
INGREDIENTS:	60ml Claytons Tonic 15ml Lime Juice dash Sugar Syrup top-up with Soda Water
GARNISH:	Thin lime slice floated in drink.
COMMENTS:	A delightful pre-dinner drink.

BELL'S BOOMER

METHOD: Build over Ice

GLASS: 470ml Fancy Hi-Ball Glass

INGREDIENTS: 30ml Berri Apple Juice
30ml Berri Orange Juice
30ml Berri Grapefruit Juice
15ml Lime Juice
120ml Dry Ginger Ale

GARNISH: Optional decoration.

COMMENTS: A large energising fruit drink, ideal before tackling those early morning breakers.

CARROT WIZZ

METHOD:	Blend with Ice and Pour
GLASS:	200ml Old Fashioned Glass
INGREDIENTS:	60ml Berri Tomato Juice 1/2 medium Carrot (thinly sliced) dash Horseradish Sauce dash Berri Lemon Juice
GARNISH:	Carrot top, floated on top
COMMENTS:	"What's up Doc?" Created by Blaza Nikolic of the Hyatt Hotel, Melbourne

CHRYSANTHEMUM

METHOD:	Build over Ice and Stir
GLASS:	290ml Salud Grande Glass
INGREDIENTS:	90ml Berri Dark Grape Juice dash Grenadine 45ml Soda Water
GARNISH:	None
COMMENTS:	The sharp classic taste of pure grape.

CLAYTONS SOUR

METHOD:	Shake with Ice and Pour
GLASS:	200ml Baccus Wine Glass
INGREDIENTS:	90ml Claytons Tonic 15ml Sugar Syrup 60ml Berri Lemon Juice
GARNISH:	Maraschino cherry
COMMENTS:	Along the traditional lines.

CLOVER BLOSSOM

METHOD: Blend with Ice and Pour

GLASS: 270ml Hi-Ball Glass

INGREDIENTS: 60ml Lemon Cordial
30ml Lime Juice
1 Egg White
dash Grenadine
top-up with Tonic Water

GARNISH: Lemon slice, mint leaf and straw.

COMMENTS: A delicate fluffy concoction.

COCK-A-DOODLE

METHOD: Shake with Ice and Strain

GLASS: 290ml Salud Grande Glass

INGREDIENTS: 90ml Berri Dark Grape Juice
90ml Berri Lemon Juice
15ml Lime Cordial
15ml Sugar Syrup
dash Grenadine

GARNISH: Lime slice and dark grapes on side of glass.

COMMENTS: Wake up to this little refresher.

CROCODILE

METHOD: Shake with Ice and Stir

GLASS: 270ml Footed Hi-Ball Glass

INGREDIENTS: 60ml Berri Grapefruit Juice
30ml Lime Juice
30ml Sugar Syrup
top-up with lemonade

GARNISH: Lime peel curl.

COMMENTS: A citrus tang makes this drink a perfect summer cooler.

DARK CLOUDS

METHOD:	Build over Ice
GLASS:	330ml Hi-Ball Glass
INGREDIENTS:	120ml Cola 60ml Claytons Tonic 60ml Dry Ginger Ale
GARNISH:	Vanilla bean and swizzle stick.
COMMENTS:	An aromatic cooler.

DICK LITTLE

METHOD:	Build over Ice
GLASS:	350ml Fancy Hi-Ball Glass
INGREDIENTS:	60ml Berri Apricot Nectar 15ml Lime Juice top-up with Bitter Lemon
GARNISH:	Lemon slices on side of glass, swizzle stick and straw.
COMMENTS:	A sharp appertising drink.

GATOR

METHOD:	Build over Ice
GLASS:	170ml Champagne Flute
INGREDIENTS:	90ml Berri Grapefruit Juice 30ml Lime Cordial
GARNISH:	Lime peel curl.
COMMENTS:	Sharp and tangy aperitif.

GINGER MICK

METHOD: Stir with Ice

GLASS: 290ml Old Fashioned Glass

INGREDIENTS: 120ml Dry Ginger Ale
15ml Lime Juice
30ml Claytons Tonic
30ml Berri Lemon Juice
60ml Berri Apple Juice

GARNISH: Apple peel threaded inside glass, with lemon slice on side with mint sprig.

COMMENTS: A thirst quenching drink to combat the summer sun.

HENRY VIII

METHOD:	Build over Ice
GLASS:	210ml Old Fashioned Glass
INGREDIENTS:	60ml Berri Apple Juice 15ml Berri Lemon Juice top-up with Dry Ginger Ale 1/2 teaspoon of Grenadine
GARNISH:	To finish, gently add Grenadine to top
COMMENTS:	A very piquant and gingery drink, suitable for afternoon relaxation.

ISLAND PARADISE

METHOD:	Shake with Ice and Strain
GLASS:	90ml Martini Glass
INGREDIENTS	30ml Berri Orange Juice 15ml Coconut Cream 30ml Lime Juice dash Sugar Syrup
GARNISH:	Lime slice and sprig of mint.
COMMENTS:	Tropical tastes in a short and piquant quencher.

JIMMY'S BEACH CRUISER

METHOD: Blend with Ice and Pour

GLASS: 380ml Viva Grande Glass

INGREDIENTS: 6 Raspberries
2 tablespoons Crushed Pineapple
60ml Berri Orange Juice
top-up with Lemonade

GARNISH: Two raspberries on side of glass, plus optional decoration.

COMMENTS: A great blend of flavours.

JUICE COMBO

METHOD: Build over Ice and Stir

GLASS: 270ml Footed Hi-Ball Glass

INGREDIENTS: 45ml Berri Pineapple Juice
45ml Berri Orange Juice
45ml Berri Apple Juice
45ml Berri Dark Grape Juice
30ml Lime Juice
15ml Sugar Syrup

GARNISH: Two dark table grapes on side of glass

COMMENTS: A refreshing blend of juices.

JULIE'S BLACK CAT

METHOD:	Build over Ice
GLASS:	270ml Hi-Ball Glass
INGREDIENTS:	15ml Berri Lemon Juice 120ml Berri Dark Grape Juice 60ml Lemonade 60ml Dry Ginger Ale
GARNISH:	Lemon twists dropped in glass, straw and optional decoration.
COMMENTS:	Let this one cross your path, a dry tasty drink.

LAVENDER

METHOD: Shake with Ice and Strain

GLASS: 210ml Old Fashioned Glass

INGREDIENTS: 90ml Berri Dark Grape Juice
15ml Berri Lemon Juice
15ml Sugar Syrup
top-up with soda water

GARNISH: Several red table grapes and lemon slice.

COMMENTS: A lightly "grapsy" drink which is most refreshing before a meal.

LAZER ZAP

METHOD: Shake with Ice and Pour

GLASS: 260ml Margarita Glass

INGREDIENTS: 30ml Berri Lemon Juice
teaspoon Honey
60ml Berri Grapefruit Juice
top-up with Soda Water

GARNISH: Lemon slice, floated.

COMMENTS: Grab your spacesuits, it will zap you out of this world.

LETHAL WEAPON

METHOD: Build over Ice and Stir

GLASS: 310ml Hi-Ball Glass

INGREDIENTS: 210ml V8 Juice
1 teaspoon Chilli Sauce
Salt and Pepper
15ml Berri Lemon Juice

GARNISH: Celery stalk

COMMENTS: Full of vitamins, but with a firey bite at the end. A great heart starter at breakfast time.

MINTLUP

METHOD:	Build over Ice
GLASS:	310ml Hi-Ball Glass
INGREDIENTS:	large sprig of Crushed Mint 15ml Lime Juice 90ml Dry Ginger Ale 90ml Lemon & Lime Mineral Water
GARNISH:	Mint leaf on lemon slice
COMMENTS:	Southern hospitality in prohibition days perhaps.

MOCKTINI

METHOD:	Stir with Ice and Strain
GLASS:	90ml Martini Glass
INGREDIENTS:	15ml Lime Juice dash Berri Lemon Juice 60ml Tonic Water
GARNISH:	A green olive on a toothpick or a lemon twist.
COMMENTS:	The classic cocktail, non-alcoholic version.

MOCQUIRI

METHOD:	Blend with Ice and Strain
GLASS:	90ml Martini Glass
INGREDIENTS:	60ml Berri Apple Juice 15ml Berri Lemon Juice 15ml Sugar Syrup
GARNISH:	Lemon or lime twist
COMMENTS:	An apple flavoured Mocktail Daiquiri

ORAMATO

METHOD:	Shake with Ice and Pour
GLASS:	240ml Footed Hi-Ball Glass
INGREDIENTS:	90ml Berri Tomato Juice 130ml Berri Orange Juice
GARNISH:	Orange peel curl.
COMMENTS:	Try this orange tomato for a taste difference.

PASSIONATE

METHOD:	Blend with Ice and Pour
GLASS:	230ml Hurricane Glass
INGREDIENTS:	teaspoon Passionfruit Pulp 60ml Berri Grapefruit Juice dash Lime Juice dash Grenadine top-up with Mineral Water
GARNISH:	Lime slice on side of glass.
COMMENTS:	Wait for the after tang!

PEACH MAGIC

METHOD: Blend with Ice and Pour

GLASS: 440ml Hurricane Glass

INGREDIENTS: 1 Peach or Apricot, stoned
90ml Berri Orange and Mango Juice
90ml Berri Apple Juice
top-up with Dry Ginger Ale

GARNISH: Watermelon slice and stemmed maraschino cherry.

COMMENTS: A large refreshing taste of the orchard

SHRINKING VIOLET

METHOD:	Build over Ice and Stir
GLASS:	270ml Hi-Ball Glass
INGREDIENTS:	120ml Berri Dark Grape Juice 90ml Lemonade 15ml Lime Juice
GARNISH:	Two dark grapes and straw
COMMENTS:	A light but sharp drink

SPAZZ

METHOD: Blend with Ice and Pour

GLASS: 310ml Hi-Ball Glass

INGREDIENTS: 1/2 Peach or Apricot, stoned
150ml Berri Pineapple Juice
15ml Lime Juice

GARNISH: Pour a teaspoon Grenadine over top of drink, add apricot slice and straw.

COMMENTS: A long, delicately flavoured drink.

STRAWBERRY ZAPPLE

METHOD: Blend with Ice and Pour

GLASS: 310ml Hi-Ball Glass

INGREDIENTS: 4 Strawberries
180ml Berri Apple Juice
30ml Berri Lemon Juice
dash Lime Cordial

GARNISH: Small strawberry on straw.

COMMENTS: A sharp, tasty, refresher.

SUNDOWNER

METHOD:	Shake with Ice and Pour
GLASS:	210ml Old Fashioned Glass
INGREDIENTS:	75ml Berri Orange and Mango Juice 15ml Berri Lemon Juice 45ml Claytons Tonic
GARNISH:	Lemon slice, floated.
COMMENTS:	A citrus tang to activate the taste buds

SYDNEY SIDER

METHOD: Shake with Ice and Pour

GLASS: 350ml Fiesta Grande Glass

INGREDIENTS: 30ml Berri Lemon Juice
30ml Berri Orange Juice
30ml Berri Grapefruit Juice
30ml Berri Pineapple Juice
60ml Berri Apple Juice
1/2 Egg White
dash Grenadine

GARNISH: Apple fan.

COMMENTS: Fruit medley in the Opera House. Created by Anthony Carroll of The Manor House Restaurant, Balmain.

TASSIE SHOT

METHOD:	Shake wih Ice and Pour
GLASS:	200ml Old Fashioned Glass
INGREDIENTS:	120ml Berri Apple Juice 60ml Berri Grapefruit Juice Sachet Lite-n-low
GARNISH:	Straw through slice of apple on top
COMMENTS:	The apple of your eye

VIRGIN MARIA

METHOD:	Blend with Ice and Pour
GLASS:	270ml Footed Hi-Ball Glass
INGREDIENTS:	180ml Berri Tomato Juice dash Berri Lemon Juice 15ml Chilli Sauce
GARNISH:	Cucumber slice, cherry tomatoes and optional decoration.
COMMENTS:	A very hot and spicey drink, guaranteed to keep you that way.

VIRGIN MARY

METHOD:	Build over Ice and Stir
GLASS:	270ml Hi-Ball Glass
INGREDIENTS:	150ml Berri Tomato Juice 15ml Berri Lemon Juice teaspoon Worcestershire Sauce 2 or 3 drops Tabasco Sauce Salt and Pepper to taste
GARNISH:	Celery stalk, lemon slice and straws
COMMENTS:	A spicey refreshing start to the day.

WEST COAST SPLASH

METHOD: Shake with Ice and Pour

GLASS: 290ml Salud Grande Glass

INGREDIENTS: 6 Mint Leaves
60ml Berri Orange and Mango Juice
top-up with Dry Ginger Ale

GARNISH: Mint leaves, plus optional decoration.

COMMENTS: This drink will certainly "dry" you off.

WITCH'S KISS

METHOD: Shake with Ice and Pour

GLASS: 330ml Hi-Ball Glass

INGREDIENTS: 150ml Berri Tropical Fruit Juice
dash Berri Lemon Juice
dash Sugar Syrup
15ml Grenadine
top-up with Soda Water

GARNISH: Lemon slice on side of glass, serve with straws and optional decoration.

COMMENTS: A light tropical flavour.

Chapter 2

SWEET

Generally sweetened to
some degree with sugar or
sugar like products,
or have a large
sweet fruit juice component.
Best suited for
consumption towards
the end of a meal,
or maybe for those of us
with a sweet tooth.

APRICOT SUPREME

METHOD:	Shake with Ice and Pour
GLASS:	270ml Hi-Ball Glass
INGREDIENTS:	150ml Berri Apricot Nectar 60ml Berri Orange Juice 15ml Berri Lemon Juice
GARNISH:	Orange slice, mint leaves and straw.
COMMENTS:	The sweet fruit alternative.

BANANA BERRY SMOOTHY

METHOD:	Blend with Ice and Pour
GLASS:	170ml Champagne Flute
INGREDIENTS:	1/3 ripe Banana 60ml Berri Orange Juice 3 tablespoons Mixed Berries
GARNISH:	Wedge banana and straw
COMMENTS:	Berry bonanza.

BE BOP A DO DA

METHOD: Blend with Ice and Pour

GLASS: 200ml Baccus Wine Glass

INGREDIENTS: 1/2 ripe Banana
tablespoon Passionfruit Pulp
tablespoon Crushed Pineapple
15ml Berri Lemon Juice

GARNISH: Long pineapple wedge and optional decoration.

COMMENTS: A thick and very tasty, tropical drink.

BEE STING

METHOD:	Blend with Ice and Strain
GLASS:	200ml Old Fashioned Glass
INGREDIENTS:	90ml Berri Apple Juice 30ml Berri Orange Juice 2 teaspoons Honey 15ml Lime Juice
GARNISH:	Sugar frosted apple slice
COMMENTS:	Sweet nectar from the bee hive

BELL'S BEACH

METHOD:	Blend with Ice and Pour
GLASS:	650ml Hurricane Glass
INGREDIENTS:	100ml Berri Orange Juice 100ml Berri Pineapple Juice 1/2 Egg White top-up with Lemonade
GARNISH:	None
COMMENTS:	A giant fluffy fruit juice.

BOBBY DAZZLER

METHOD: Blend Grenadine with Ice and Pour

GLASS: 290ml Poco Grande Glass

INGREDIENTS: 60ml Grenadine
200ml Cola
Whipped Cream
Hundreds and Thousands

GARNISH: Pour into glass, top with whipped cream and sprinkle with hundreds and thousands. Place strawberry on side and serve with swizzle stick and straw

COMMENTS: By Maxine Nash, Bubbles-Wodonga Hotel, was a runner-up in the Best Border BeverageCompetition of 1991

CANE TOAD

METHOD: Shake with Ice and Pour

GLASS: 220ml Fancy Hi-Ball Glass

INGREDIENTS: 30ml Passionfruit Pulp
30ml Sugar Syrup
30ml Berri Lemon Juice
top-up with Dry Ginger Ale

GARNISH: Two lemon slices and mint leaves

COMMENTS: A fizzy cane toad without the poison, a very refreshing tarty drink.

CHAMPAGNE MOCKTAIL

METHOD:	Build over Ice
GLASS:	260ml Tulip Champagne Flute
INGREDIENTS:	Sugar Cube 30ml Berri Apple Juice 120ml Lemon-Lime Mineral Water
GARNISH:	Optional decoration.
COMMENTS:	Cool summer refresher.

CORIO BAY SUNSET

METHOD:	Blend with Ice and Strain
GLASS:	330ml Hi-Ball Glass
INGREDIENTS:	4 large Strawberries 30ml Lime Juice 120ml Berri Orange and Mango Juice 15ml Claytons Tonic top-up with Lemonade
GARNISH:	Orange slice
COMMENTS:	A delightful combination of citrus and berry flavours.

DOCTOR'S ORDERS

METHOD:	Shake with Ice and Strain
GLASS:	290ml Salud Grande Glass
INGREDIENTS:	30ml Lime Juice 120ml Berri Grapefruit Juice 2 sachets Lite-n-Low top-up with Tonic Water
GARNISH:	Lime slice and straws.
COMMENTS:	A juice a day to keep the doctor away.

DUST SETTLER

METHOD: Blend with Ice and Pour

GLASS: 290ml Poco Grande Glass

INGREDIENTS: 90ml Crushed Pineapple
90ml Berri Apple Juice
top-up with Lemonade

GARNISH: Apple slice

COMMENTS: Sweet and smooth, guaranteed to settle the dust.

FRENZEE

METHOD:	Blend with Ice and Pour
GLASS:	380ml Viva Grande Glass
INGREDIENTS:	3 large Strawberries sachet Lite-n-Low 60ml Pineapple Yoghurt 60ml Berri Pineapple Juice top-up with Soda Water
GARNISH:	Punch straw through strawberry and sit it in the glass
COMMENTS:	Tropical dairy delight.

FRUIT MOCQUIRI

METHOD: Blend with Ice and Pour

GLASS: 260ml Margarita Glass

INGREDIENTS: 60ml Strawberries, Peaches or Mango
15ml Sugar Syrup
15ml Berri Lemon Juice
30ml Berri Apple Juice

GARNISH: Small slice of the ingredient fruit

COMMENTS: A smooth rich blend of your favourit fruit. I particularly like mango, as used in the photograph above.

FRUIT SQUASH

METHOD:	Blend with Ice and Pour
GLASS:	330ml Hi-Ball Glass
INGREDIENTS:	2 Strawberries 4 Raspberries tablespoon Crushed Pineapple tablespoon Passionfruit Pulp 1/2 Kiwi Fruit 60ml Berri Orange Juice
GARNISH:	Berry studded pineapple spear.
COMMENTS:	A fruit lovers delight.

HEALTH FARM

METHOD: Blend with Ice and Pour

GLASS: 270ml Hi-Ball Glass

INGREDIENTS: 90ml Berri Pineapple Juice
2 slices Cantaloupe Melon
90ml Berri Orange Juice
2 teaspoons Honey
1/2 ripe Banana

GARNISH: Cantaloupe wedge and swizzle stick.

COMMENTS: A great drink for the health conscious. Created by Wayne Baker of Tousson Restaurant, Geelong.

IRON MAN

METHOD:	Blend with Ice and Pour
GLASS:	350ml Fancy Hi-Ball Glass
INGREDIENTS:	1 Egg 45ml Honey 1 ripe Banana, sliced 150ml Berri Orange Juice
GARNISH:	A vanilla bean floated, then sprinkle flake chocolate over top.
COMMENTS:	Choc-a-block with energy. Created by Rowan Sapwell, Manager, Fishermen's Pier Restaurant Geelong

KATE'S PINK ECHIDNA

METHOD: Blend with Ice and Pour

GLASS: 310ml Hi-Ball Glass

INGREDIENTS: 3 Strawberries
2 slices Cantaloupe Melon
30ml Sugar Syrup
dash Berri Lemon Juice
top-up with Lemonade

GARNISH: Cantaloupe slice and small strawberry on side of glass.

COMMENTS: A delicate melon flavour.

LEMON FIZZ

METHOD:	Build over Ice
GLASS:	260ml Champagne Tulip Flute
INGREDIENTS:	180ml Lemonade 30ml Berri Lemon Juice scoop Lemon Gelati
GARNISH:	Lemon slice and Italian flag
COMMENTS:	A sweet lemon sensation.

MATT'S CLASSIC

METHOD: Blend with Ice and Pour

GLASS: 260ml Tulip Champagne Flute

INGREDIENTS:
3 Strawberries
1/2 Kiwi Fruit
60ml Plain Yoghurt
60ml Berri Apricot Nectar
15ml Sugar Syrup

GARNISH: Kiwi slice on side of glass.

COMMENTS: A thick fruity blend with a gentle hint of apricots.

MELON DELIGHT

METHOD:	Blend with Ice and Pour
GLASS:	270ml Hi-Ball Glass
INGREDIENTS:	4 tablespoons Watermelon 2 tablespoons Rockmelon 2 tablespoons Honeydew Melon 30ml Berri Lemon Juice 2 teaspoons Honey
GARNISH:	1 ball of each of the melons.
COMMENTS:	A summer delight. Created by Peter Podbury of Savvas Restaurant, Geelong.

MICKEY MOUSE

METHOD: Build over Ice

GLASS: 270ml Hi-Ball Glass

INGREDIENTS: 90ml Berri Orange Juice
30ml Raspberry Cordial
90ml Lemonade

GARNISH: Two cherries on side of glass.

COMMENTS: A dash of vitamin C for you sweet tooth people.

PARADISE QUENCHER

METHOD:	Blend with Ice and Pour
GLASS:	310ml Hi-Ball Glass
INGREDIENTS:	1/3 small Banana slice Mango 60ml Berri Orange and Mango Juice top-up with Lemonade
GARNISH:	Banana and mango slices on side of glass, serve with straws.
COMMENTS:	The sweet succulent flavours of tropical fruit.

QUEENSLAND CRUSH

METHOD:	Blend with Ice and Pour
GLASS:	270ml Hi-Ball Glass
INGREDIENTS:	150ml Berri Orange Juice 3 tablespoons Crushed Pineapple 15ml Berri Lemon Juice 15ml Sugar Syrup
GARNISH:	Pineapple wedge, orange slice
COMMENTS:	A tropical refresher.

QUENCHIE

METHOD:	Build over Ice and Stir
GLASS:	390ml Poco Grande Glass
INGREDIENTS:	150ml Berri Orange Juice 150ml Lemonade 2 desertspoons Passionfruit Pulp
GARNISH:	Slice of orange, slice of lemon with 2 marashino cherries on toothpicks, serve with swizzle sticks and straws.
COMMENTS:	Created by Maxine Nash of Bubbles-Wodonga Hotel, was runner-up in the Best Border Beverage Competition of 1991.

RED MAGIC

METHOD: Blend with Ice and Strain

GLASS: 290ml Salud Grande Glass

INGREDIENTS: 90ml Berri Apple Juice
4 Raspberries
1 teaspoon Honey

GARNISH: Raspberries on side of glass, with a little mint.

COMMENTS: You will "bee" pleasantly surprised.

SHIRLEY TEMPLE

METHOD: Build over Ice

GLASS: 310ml Hi-Ball Glass

INGREDIENTS: 15ml Grenadine
Ginger Ale or Lemonade

GARNISH: Slice of orange, serve with swizzle stick and two straws.

COMMENTS: For a tangy variation to this Mocktail try a Shirley Temple No 2. Use the following: 60ml Berri Pineapple Juice to a glass half full of ice. Top with Lemonade, float 15ml Passionfruit pulp on top and garnish with pineapple wedge and cherry.

SUNBURNT KIWI

METHOD: Blend with Ice and Pour

GLASS: 440ml Hurricane Glass

INGREDIENTS: 1 ripe Plum, stoned
1 Kiwi Fruit, skinned
15ml Berri Lemon Juice
60ml Berri Dark Grape Juice
top-up with Lemonade

GARNISH: Slice of kiwi fruit on side of glass.

COMMENTS: A thick, rich drink from New Zealand.

SURF COAST SUNSET

METHOD: Build over Ice and Stir

GLASS: 200ml Old Fashioned Glass

INGREDIENTS: 60ml Berri Apple Juice
60ml Berri Orange Juice
1/2 teaspoon Grenadine

GARNISH: Orange slice with cherry in the centre

COMMENTS: Add the Grenadine last and watch it sink to the bottom as the setting sun.

WALLINGTON SPECIAL

METHOD:	Blend with Ice and Pour
GLASS:	270ml Footed Hi-Ball Glass
INGREDIENTS:	6 Strawberries 180ml Berri Pineapple Juice 1/2 Egg White 15ml Sugar Syrup
GARNISH:	Small strawberry on side of glass and straw.
COMMENTS:	Tropical fruity blend.

WINDLESS HURRICANE

METHOD: Build over Ice

GLASS: 290ml Poco Grande Glass

INGREDIENTS: 180ml Berri Orange Juice
30ml Claytons Tonic
dash Berri Lemon Juice
dash Grenadine

GARNISH: Lemon, orange and maraschino cherry, plus straws and swizzle stick.

COMMENTS: A fruity tingle.

Chapter 3

CREAMY

Use cream,
milk egg white,
ice cream,
coconut milk
and coconut cream,
to give texture
and full flavour.

ANDY'S PASSION

METHOD:	Blend with Ice and Pour
GLASS:	270ml Hi-Ball Glass
INGREDIENTS:	90ml Passionfruit Pulp 90ml Berri Tropical Juice 60ml Natural Yoghurt
GARNISH:	Lime slice, swizzle stick and straw.
COMMENTS:	A taste of sunshine with the unique tang of passionfruit.

ANGEL'S KISS

METHOD: Blend with Ice and Pour

GLASS: 290ml Poco Grande Glass

INGREDIENTS: scoop Vanilla Ice Cream
tablespoon Passionfruit Pulp
150ml Berri Apricot Nectar

GARNISH: Mint leaves.

COMMENTS: A wonderful blend of passionfruit and apricots.

APRICOT SMOOTHIE

METHOD: Blend with Ice and Pour

GLASS: 390ml Poco Grande Glass

INGREDIENTS: 2 Apricots, stoned
90ml Milk
15ml Berri Lemon Juice
30ml Vanilla Yoghurt

GARNISH: Apricot slice and straws.

COMMENTS: A large smooth drink, with apricot flavour.

BANANA BASH

METHOD: Blend with Ice and Pour

GLASS: 310ml Hi-Ball Glass

INGREDIENTS: 1 ripe Banana
4 Raspberries
scoop Vanilla Ice Cream
90ml Berri Tropical Fruit Juice

GARNISH: A sugar dusted raspberry on a banana wedge.

COMMENTS: A great tasting blend of rasperry and banana.

BANANA-CHOC SHAKE

METHOD:	Blend with Ice and Pour
GLASS:	440ml Hurricane Glass
INGREDIENTS:	1 ripe Banana, sliced 2 scoops Chocolate Ice Cream 210ml Milk
GARNISH:	Teaspoon grated chocolate and straw
COMMENTS:	The biggest chocolate milkshake with a faint banana overtone.

BANANA SMOOTHY

METHOD:	Blend with Ice and Pour
GLASS:	270ml Hi-Ball Glass
INGREDIENTS:	120ml Berri Orange Juice 1 ripe Banana 30ml Sugar Syrup 30ml Cream dash Lime Juice
GARNISH:	Edge glass with banana wedge and lime slice
COMMENTS:	Smooth, healthy and sweet Mocktail

BANBERRY

METHOD:	Blend with Ice and Pour
GLASS:	200ml Baccus Wine Glass
INGREDIENTS:	4 small Strawberries 1/2 ripe Banana 90ml Milk 30ml Sugar Syrup
GARNISH:	Small strawberry on rim of glass
COMMENTS:	Thick, creamy, luscious, strawberry drink

BEN'S PLAY LUNCH

METHOD:	Blend with Ice and Pour
GLASS:	330ml Hi-Ball Glass
INGREDIENTS:	1 ripe Banana 3 tablespoons Crushed Pineapple 60ml Coconut Cream 60ml Berri Tropical Fruit Juice 15ml Berri Lemon Juice
GARNISH:	Desiccated coconut frosted glass, with optional decoration.
COMMENTS:	A thick fruity drink to assist your primate instincts.

BLUSHING BERRY

METHOD: Blend with Ice, Raspberry Cordial, Coconut Milk, Milk and Whipped Cream.

GLASS: 260ml Margarita Class

INGREDIENTS: 150ml Milk
60ml Raspberry Cordial
60ml Whipped Cream
15ml Coconut Milk
frozen Raspberries

GARNISH: Place frozen raspberries around rim.

COMMENTS: Created by Mary Jane Porta of Termo, Albury and was a finalist in the Best Border Beverage Competition of 1991

BOBBY'S BOOZE BUSTER

METHOD: Blend with Ice and Pour

GLASS: 290ml Poco Grande Glass

INGREDIENTS: 1/2 Banana
30ml Coconut Cream
50ml Berri Apple Juice
scoop Vanilla Ice Cream
sprinkle Cinnamon

GARNISH: Apple wedge and cinnamon stick.

COMMENTS: A very refreshing, slightly bitter-sweet drink.

BRAZILIAN BREAKDANCE

METHOD: Blend with Ice and Pour

GLASS: 390ml Poco Grande Glass

INGREDIENTS: 2 teaspoons Instant Coffee
scoop Vanilla Ice Cream
120ml Milk

GARNISH: Teaspoon chocolate flakes.

COMMENTS: A luscious, thick glass of iced coffee flavour, with just a hint of sweetness.

CANDY BAR

METHOD:	Blend with Ice, Milk Chocolate and Caramel Topping
GLASS:	290ml Poco Grande Glass
INGREDIENTS:	200ml Milk 15ml Chocolate Topping 30ml Caramel Topping Whipped Cream
GARNISH:	Top with whipped cream and sprinkle with icing sugar and shaved chocolate
COMMENTS:	Created by Mary Ann Marcure of Anthony's Restaurant, Wodonga and was a finalist in the Best Border Beverage Competition of 1991

CHIQUITTA

METHOD:	Blend with Ice and Strain
GLASS:	200ml Baccus Wine Glass
INGREDIENTS:	1 ripe Banana, thinly sliced 60ml Berri Orange Juice 15ml Cream dash Grenadine
GARNISH:	Orange slice with twist
COMMENTS:	The smoothie that drives you bananas.

CHOCOLATE CREAM

METHOD: Blend with Ice and Pour

GLASS: 270ml Hi-Ball Glass

INGREDIENTS: 2 teaspoons Cocoa Powder
90ml Milk
30ml Cream
60ml Sugar Syrup

GARNISH: Sprinkle cocoa powder over top.

COMMENTS: The classic chocolate temptation.

CHOCOLATE FROG

METHOD: Build over Ice

GLASS: 390ml Poco Grande Glass

INGREDIENTS: 250ml Cola
15ml Chocolate Topping
dash Peppermint Essence
Whipped Cream

GARNISH: Top with whipped cream and sprinkle with nutmeg and place sliced strawberry on side of glass. Serve with swizzle stick and straw.

COMMENTS: By Annie Brouwer of Thermo-Albury and was a runner-up in the Best Border Beverage Competition of 1991

COCO CREAM

METHOD: Shake with Ice and Strain

GLASS: 260ml Tulip Champagne Flute

INGREDIENTS: 80ml Berri Dark Grape Juice
110ml Berri Orange Juice
30ml Coconut Cream
15ml Grenadine

GARNISH: Frost glass with desiccated coconut and add maraschino cherry.

COMMENTS: A fruity Mocktail, with coconut influence.

COCOMINT

METHOD: Blend with Ice and Pour

GLASS: 270ml Hi-Ball Glass

INGREDIENTS:

scoop Chocolate Ice Cream
30ml Coconut Cream
60ml Milk
30ml Lime Cordial

GARNISH: Teaspoon crushed peppermint crisp bar, mint leaves.

COMMENTS: A rich creamy coconut-chocolate blend.

COFFEE CRUNCH

METHOD: Blend with Ice and Pour

GLASS: 440ml Hurricane Glass

INGREDIENTS: 90ml Coconut Cream
90ml Cream
1 Egg
120ml Cottees Iced Coffee

GARNISH: Sprinkle with cinnamon sugar, serve with straw and decorate as desired.

COMMENTS: Created by Gaye Fendyke of Termo-Albury and was a runner-up in the Best Border Beverage Competion of 1991.

CORRA BEAR

METHOD: Build over Ice and Stir

GLASS: 290ml Poco Grande Glass

INGREDIENTS: 200ml Cola
30ml Cottees Iced Coffee
Whipped Cream

GARNISH: Top with whipped cream and place maraschino cherry on top, with a slice of kiwi fruit on side of glass. Serve with straws.

COMMENTS: Created by Mary Jane Porta of Termo, Albury and was outright winner of the Best Border Beverages Competition of 1991.

CREAMY BANANA

METHOD:	Blend with Ice and Strain
GLASS:	350ml Fiesta Grande Glass
INGREDIENTS:	1 ripe Banana, sliced 30ml Coconut Cream 60ml Milk scoop Vanilla Ice Cream
GARNISH:	Sprinkle with chocolate flake.
COMMENTS:	A delicate creamy drink.

ISSY WASSY

METHOD: Blend with Ice and Pour

GLASS: 440ml Hurricane Glass

INGREDIENTS: 120ml Milk
1/2 Banana
2 slices Cantaloupe Melon

GARNISH: Cantaloupe slice with straws.

COMMENTS: For the smooth stylish chap

JAFFA

METHOD: Blend with Ice and Pour

GLASS: 200ml Old Fashioned Glass

INGREDIENTS: scoop Chocolate Ice Cream
90ml Berri Orange Juice

GARNISH: 1 teaspoon grated chocolate on top.

COMMENTS: Just like a liquid jaffa.

JERSEY COW

METHOD:	Stir over Ice
GLASS:	290ml Old Fashioned Glass
INGREDIENTS:	180ml Cola scoop Chocolate Ice Cream
GARNISH:	Teaspoon of grated chocolate over top
COMMENTS:	A choc-cola delight

JOH'S COUNTRY

METHOD: Blend with Ice and Pour

GLASS: 350ml Fiesta Grande Glass

INGREDIENTS: 45ml Berri Pineapple Juice
30ml Coconut Cream
dash Lime Cordial
60ml Berri Mango and Orange Juice

GARNISH: Mango slice, straw and optional decoration.

COMMENTS: Rich creamy coconut flavour.

KERRY'S ROSE GARDEN

METHOD:	Blend all ingredients except Cream, with Ice and Pour
GLASS:	290ml Salud Grande Glass
INGREDIENTS:	30ml Berri Dark Grape Juice 1 tablespoon Watermelon 15ml Berri Lemon Juice 1/2 Egg White dash Sugar Syrup
GARNISH:	Float cream, sprinkle with cinnamon
COMMENTS:	A sharp drink, with subtle flavour.

MANGOLITE

METHOD:	Blend with Ice and Pour
GLASS:	310ml Hi-Ball Glass
INGREDIENTS:	150ml Berri Mango and Orange Juice 60ml Milk dash Claytons Tonic sachet Lite-n-Low
GARNISH:	Optional decoration.
COMMENTS:	A smooth healthy drink.

MILK NOG

METHOD: Shake with Ice and Pour

GLASS: 310ml Hi-Ball Glass

INGREDIENTS: 1 Egg
200ml Milk
30ml Sugar Syrup

GARNISH: Vanilla bean, and a dusting of cinnamon

COMMENTS: Mother's favourite egg-flip for building healthy bodies.

NICK'S HEALTH DRINK

METHOD: Shake with Ice and Strain

GLASS: 290ml Poco Grande Glass

INGREDIENTS: 60ml V8 Juice
60ml Berri Orange Juice
120ml Natural Yoghurt

GARNISH: Carrot top and straw.

COMMENTS: Very definately a healthy drink.

PENINSULA PELICAN

METHOD:	Blend with Ice and Pour
GLASS:	290ml Old Fashioned Glass
INGREDIENTS:	90ml Berri Apple Juice 1/2 Egg White 2 teaspoons Honey
GARNISH:	Straws and optional decoration.
COMMENTS:	Sweet treat before that moonlight stroll

PINA CON NADA

METHOD: Blend with Ice and Pour

GLASS: 270ml Footed Hi-Ball Glass

INGREDIENTS: 90ml Berri Pineapple Juice
30ml Coconut Cream
15ml Sugar Syrup

GARNISH: Wedge of pineapple and a strawberry with straws.

COMMENTS: The creamy non-alcoholic version of the famous Pina Colada.

PINK FROTH

METHOD:	Blend with Ice and Pour
GLASS:	490ml Fiesta Grande Glass
INGREDIENTS:	60ml Cream 45ml Sugar Syrup 15ml Grenadine 15ml Berri Lemon Juice 15ml Lime Juice top-up with Lemonade
GARNISH:	Optional decoration
COMMENTS:	Sweet creamy and smooooooth.

SILVER QUEEN

METHOD:	Build over Ice
GLASS:	170ml Tulip Champagne Flute
INGREDIENTS:	90ml Sparkling White Grape Juice scoop Vanilla Ice Cream
GARNISH:	Several white table grapes
COMMENTS:	A wine spider (non-alcoholic of course)

STRAWBERRY SPIDER

METHOD:	Blend with Ice all ingredients except Lemonade and Ice Cream
GLASS:	300ml Footed Hi-Ball Glass
INGREDIENTS:	6 small Strawberries 15ml Sugar Syrup 90ml Lemonade scoop Strawberry Ice Cream
GARNISH:	Pour blended ingredients in glass, almost fill with lemonade, then top-up with strawberry ice cream. Place small whole strawberry on side.
COMMENTS:	Children's favourite

SUNSHINE

METHOD:	Blend with Ice and Pour
GLASS:	270ml Hi-Ball Glass
INGREDIENTS:	90ml Berri Pineapple Juice 30ml Coconut Cream 1/2 Banana 30ml Cream 30ml Sugar Syrup
GARNISH:	Wedge of pineapple and one cherry. Serve with swizzle stick and straw.
COMMENTS:	Created by Maxine Nash of Bubbles-Wodonga Hotel, was a runner-up in Best Border Beverage Competition of 1991.

TROPICAL RAIN

METHOD: Blend with Ice and Pour

GLASS: 330ml Hi-Ball Glass

INGREDIENTS: tablespoon Passionfruit Pulp
120ml Berri Pineapple Juice
1/2 ripe Mango
30ml Plain Yoghurt
dash Grenadine

GARNISH: Mango slices and raspberry on tooth-pick on side of glass.

COMMENTS: A thick tropical drink, with the tarty flavour of passionfruit.

Acknowledgements

The publishers wish to thank the following sponsors, without whose help this book would not have been possible.

Berrivale Orchards Ltd.
39-40 Dequetteville Terrace, Kent Town SA 5067
Special thanks to: Mr. Andrew Ralph, National Marketing Manager
Suppliers of: Berri Orange Juice, Berri Mango & Orange Juice, Berri Dark Grape Juice, Berri Lemon Juice, Berri Tropical Juice, Berri Apricot Nectar, Berri Peach Nectar, Berri Tomato Juice, Berri Apple Juice, Berri Pineapple Juice

SSB Advertising Pty. Ltd.
18 Ruthven Avenue, Adelaide SA 5000
Special thanks to: Mr. Peter Ivett, Managing Director

Phillip Lazarus - Australian Agent for Libbey Glass of America
Cnr. Beauchamp Rd & McPherson St. Matraville NSW 2036
Suppliers of: A wide range of quality glassware to the retail and hospitality trade.

AC/Crown Glassware Ltd.
816 Bourke St. Waterloo NSW 2017
Suppliers of: A diverse range of glassware especially designed for the hospitality industry.

Alpen Products Pty. Ltd.
130 Old Pittwater Road, Brookvale NSW 2100
Suppliers of: Party novelties, decorations, toothpicks, swizzle sticks and other drink and party accessories.

Ms. Julie Haynes, Reginal Project Co-Ordinator
North East Drug and Alcohol Services
and convener of the Best Border Beverages Competion

Mr. David Anderson, Director-Road Safety
Vicroads, 290 Burwood Road, Hawthorn, Victoria 3122

Mr. Chris Suhr, Advance Certificate Co-Ordinater
Gordon TAFE College
For developing and editing recipes in this book, his devotion to the cause can never be fully appreciated.
Mr.Rowan Sapwell, Manager, Fishermen's Pier Restaurant, Geelong.
Without Rowan's assistance in the origination of many of the recipes, this book may not have been possible.
Ms. Katrina Hunt, Ms. Sue Minchinton and Mr. Demetris Avraam, of Fishermen's Pier Restaurant, Geelong
We thank them for their tireless enthusiasm and assistance in the development of the recipes in this book.

INDEX

Page

APERITIF OR DRY

INDEX

Page

SWEET

INDEX

Page

CREAMY

This book is stocked by all good booksellers and liquor retailers, however, if you have difficulty obtaining additional copies then please return this order form. Other books in the 101 Series may be ordered using this form, just note title and send payment for the required amount. All books in the 101 Series are $9.95 plus $1.50 P & P. Note that for orders of more than five copies no postage or packaging is payable as at 31st December 1991 (Prices subject to change without notice)

R & R Publishing, P.O. Box 1071, Epping, NSW 2121
12 Treeview Place, Epping, NSW 2121
Telephone Orders: (02) 876 5958 Fax (02) 876 3782

Please send me .... copy/ies of book/s as marked @ $9.95 plus $1.50 post and packaging per copy.
Find enclosed my cheque/money order for $................. or charge my credit card

EXPIRY DATE .... SIGNATURE ....

BANKCARD/MASTERCARD/VISA

| | | | |–| | | | | | | | | | | | |

NAME: ______________________________

ADDRESS ______________________________

______________________________ P/CODE ________

☐ 101 Mocktails
☐
☐
☐

MIX IT
THE BEST